Turtle Trouble

Written by Lynette Evans

Mexico

My name is Maria. I live in Mexico City, the capital of Mexico. Scientists figure there are more than a million sea-turtle nests on Mexico's soft, sandy beaches. Do you know why people try to look after these buried eggs?

Contents

A Journey Through Time	4
Ocean Giants	6
The Seven Sea Turtles	8
Long-Distance Swimmers	10
Nighttime Nesters	12
Run for the Sea!	14
Human Impact	16
Science to the Rescue	18
Working Together	20
Friends from Afar	22
Find Out More!	24
Index	24

Look for the **Activity Zone!**
When you see this picture, you will find an activity to try.

A Journey Through Time

Turtles are easy to recognize because of their bony shells. Scientists have found evidence to show that they have lived on Earth since the days of the dinosaurs.

There are many kinds of turtles. Some are tiny, and some are huge. Some live on land, some live in fresh water, and some live in the sea. Their tough, scaly skin and strong shells help keep them safe. Their bodies, shells, and flippers are all shaped to help them move around.

Carapace (upper part of the shell)

Streamlined shell joined to backbone and covered with hornlike plates, called *scutes*

A SEA TURTLE

Plastron (lower part of the shell)

Four flipperlike legs

evidence   something that helps a person figure out the facts

For safety, this turtle has tucked its legs and neck into its shell. All turtles except sea turtles can do this.

What Are Reptiles?

Turtles are reptiles. Scientists describe reptiles in the following ways.

- All reptiles are cold-blooded. (They rely on the warmth of the sun to heat their bodies.)

- All reptiles are vertebrates. (They have a backbone, or spine.)

- All reptiles have scaly skin.

- All reptiles breathe air.

- Almost all reptiles lay eggs.

The animals below are also reptiles.

Eyes

Powerful jaw (no teeth)

Snake

Lizard

Crocodile

5

Ocean Giants

Sea turtles are the largest turtles of all. They spend most of their lives swimming alone in warm ocean currents. Some graze on sea grasses and seaweed. Others feed on jellyfish, shrimp, crabs, or other small sea creatures.

Sea turtles are strong, graceful swimmers and excellent deep-sea divers. Although they can stay underwater for a long time, they must swim to the surface to breathe air. Thousands of sea turtles once surfed the ocean currents. Today, all sea turtles are endangered.

endangered   an animal that could die out because so few are left

Living in Two Worlds

Sea turtles sleep on the surface of deep water or under rocks in shallow water. Their heartbeat slows so they do not have to breathe very often.

Sea turtles come out of the water and onto land to breed. Folktales tell of sea turtles crying when they leave the ocean. However, sea turtles only appear to cry because of the salty water and food they live on. Their bodies produce salty "tears" to get rid of extra salt. The tears wash away when the turtles are in the sea, but on land, they look like real tears.

Leatherback turtle

The warm coastal waters and the soft, sandy beaches of Mexico are home to all but one kind of the world's sea turtles.

The Seven Sea Turtles

There are seven species of sea turtles. Scientists identify each species by the special features of their shells and flippers. They learn more about sea turtles by observing and recording the appearance and behaviors of each species. Additionally, scientists collect information about the size, diet, and home, or habitat, of each species.

Sea turtles can live to be more than 100 years old!

Flatback

Size: $3\frac{1}{4}$ feet
Diet: sea cucumbers, jellyfish, seaweed
Habitat: bays, shallow water
- It is found only near Australia and Papua New Guinea.

Leatherback

Size: 4–6 feet
Diet: jellyfish
Habitat: open ocean
- It is the only sea turtle that does not have a hard shell.
- It is the largest living turtle.

species a group of similar animals that can have babies

Loggerhead

Size: $2\frac{1}{2} - 3\frac{1}{2}$ feet
Diet: shellfish, crabs
Habitat: coastal bays
- It is named for its large head and strong jaws.

Kemp's ridley

Size: 2 feet
Diet: crabs, clams, mussels, shrimp
Habitat: shallow, muddy waters

Green sea turtle

Size: $3\frac{1}{2} - 4$ feet
Diet: sea grass, algae
Habitat: coastal bays
- It is the only sea turtle that does not eat meat as an adult.

Hawksbill

Size: $2\frac{1}{2} - 3$ feet
Diet: sponges, anemones, squid, shrimp
Habitat: coastal bays, rocky reefs
- This turtle lives in tropical waters.

Olive ridley

Size: $2 - 2\frac{1}{2}$ feet
Diet: crabs, shrimp, fish
Habitat: coastal bays, sometimes open ocean
- It is named for its olive-green shell.

Long-Distance Swimmers

Each year, sea turtles **migrate** hundreds or even thousands of miles across the ocean. They swim from their feeding grounds back to the exact beach on which they hatched. There, they breed and then make the long journey back again.

Scientists are still working to understand how sea turtles find their way in water. In the open ocean, there are no landmarks to guide the turtles, and they must battle strong ocean currents to stay on course.

migrate to travel to different places at different times of the year

Olive ridley turtles nest on the beaches of Baja California, Mexico. They swim all the way from their feeding grounds in Japan. Long ago, thousands of these turtles would gather in the waters off the beaches. Today, they are a rare sight.

Scientists at Work

Scientists who study ocean plants and animals are called *marine biologists*. Like all scientists, they begin their research with a question. Finding the answer is a little like working on a jigsaw puzzle. It can take many people many years to build the whole picture. With each piece of new information, the picture changes.

Scientists call the different ideas they form along the way *theories*. One theory about how sea turtles find their way is that they use Earth's magnetic field to guide them.

Earth's magnetic field the magnetic forces in and around Earth

Nighttime Nesters

During the summer months, large groups of sea turtles gather in the warm waters off the nesting beaches. Most males never leave the water, but in the cool and dark of night, the females drag their heavy bodies up onto land to dig nests and lay eggs.

The body features that make sea turtles successful in the water make them slow and put them at risk on land. It is important never to bother a nesting turtle.

Step by Step

> The leatherback is the only sea turtle known to make a sound. It gurgles and rumbles as it builds its nest.

Green turtle covering her eggs

1. Building the Nest
The female turtle crawls over the sand until she finds a safe spot. She scoops away loose sand with her front flippers; then she turns her body and uses her back flippers to dig a deep, narrow hole.

2. Laying the Eggs
The turtle drops two or three eggs at a time into the hole. The eggs have a tough, leathery shell, so they do not crack when they fall. There can be 80 to 100 eggs in a clutch!

3. Burying the Eggs
The turtle pushes sand over the eggs with her rear flippers. She packs the sand down and uses her front flippers to fling sand around so that the nest is well hidden. Then she returns to the sea.

clutch   all the eggs or young in one nest

Run for the Sea!

It takes about two months for sea-turtle eggs to incubate. If the sand is hot, the babies grow faster, and they will be mostly females. Cooler sand produces a greater number of male turtles.

Sea-turtle babies, or hatchlings, dig their way out of their nest as a group. Once up on the sand, they turn toward the sea. Then they run for their lives! If they reach the water safely, they swim as fast as they can for about a day and a half until they are in the deep, open ocean.

incubate   to allow the baby animal inside the egg to grow until it is ready to hatch

Danger, Beware!

Sea-turtle hatchlings face many natural dangers such as

- "drowning" in soft sand.
- overheating in the sun.
- hungry, circling birds.
- hungry crabs ready to snatch and grab.
- sharks waiting in the water.

Only one baby turtle in every thousand **survives** to be an adult.

Sea-turtle hatchlings appear to vanish once they reach the sea. Scientists think they float along, hidden in seaweed.

Life Cycle of a Sea Turtle

Adult

Egg in clutch

Hatchling

Young, or juvenile, sea turtle

survive   to stay alive

15

Human Impact

Sea turtles face many dangers in nature, but it is the actions of humans that have nearly made sea turtles extinct. Each year, thousands of turtles drown when they become tangled in fishing nets. Others die from swallowing plastic bags floating in the ocean.

In some parts of the world, people harvest sea turtles for their meat, eggs, shells, and skin. The Mexican government made collecting sea-turtle eggs illegal in 1971 and killing sea turtles illegal in 1990. However, illegal harvesting is still a big problem.

This young hawksbill is being set free from a fishing net. Sadly, many others are not so lucky.

extinct   when a plant or animal no longer exists because it has died out

Sea-turtle hatchlings know to head toward the ocean, because at night it is a lighter color than the sand. However, if the lights on buildings are brighter than the ocean, the hatchlings can head in the wrong direction.

Turtle Products

In many countries, sea turtles are now protected by law. However, in some places, people still make and sell jewelry and ornaments made from the beautiful shells of sea turtles. They eat turtle eggs and use leathery turtle skin to make handbags, shoes, and belts. Many tourists buy turtle products without thinking about the animals that were harmed to create those products. Their actions put the future of turtles at risk.

Science to the Rescue

Scientists are working hard to understand more about these endangered animals. The facts they gather from their studies help people plan different ways to help. By counting turtles, scientists can figure out how many are left. These facts help convince others that they need to help, too.

In Mexico, there are now laws to control nighttime lighting on the beaches where turtles nest. Shrimpers must have a special device in their nets so that sea turtles can swim free.

This shrimp net has a special metal grid in it that keeps turtles from being caught in the catch.

Nesting Black Turtles at Colola, Mexico

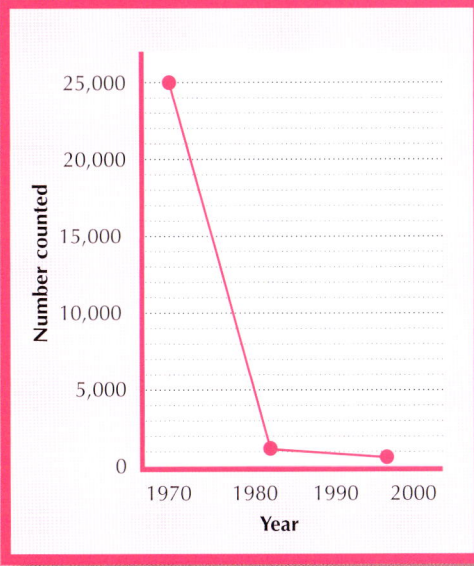

Turtle Tech-Talk

Satellite transmitters are a very useful way of keeping an eye on sea turtles. Using computer-mapping systems, scientists can see where the turtles migrate, what routes they travel, and how fast they swim. This helps scientists learn where feeding grounds are located and what dangers turtles face at sea.

Transmitter (glued to carapace, falls off in 8–10 months)

Marine biologists, such as George Balazs, shown here, capture sea turtles to measure and weigh them. They attach a metal ID tag to a flipper on each turtle and then put the turtle back in the sea.

satellite transmitter a device that sends out a signal that can be tracked

Working Together

Many people around the world want to help save sea turtles. It takes commitment and teamwork to save an endangered animal. Scientists often work with people from local communities to make sure that they know about the problem. They encourage locals to join them in saving sea turtles. Volunteers often patrol beaches to keep nesting turtles safe. Some fishermen become valuable guides for scientists on the lookout for sea turtles to track and study.

Whenever people are careful to keep oceans and beaches free of trash, poisons, and pollution, they help protect sea turtles.

volunteer   someone who helps without being paid

Small Hands Help, Too!

Projecto TAMAR Turtle Conservation Center in Brazil is run by Guy and Maria Marcovaldi. They have saved more than 2,000 sea turtles.

At the Projecto TAMAR Turtle Conservation Center, local children learn how to help sea turtles. Even a young child can help a sea-turtle hatchling reach the ocean safely.

These people are scouts doing volunteer work. They are helping scientists measure leatherback turtles in Costa Rica.

21

Friends from Afar

Tourists often play an important part in sea-turtle survival. When people travel into an area to enjoy the scenery and the wildlife, they often visit national parks and animal reserves. The money they spend at these places helps keep the parks operating and the endangered animals protected. The earnings from ecotourism also help fund scientific studies so that people can keep track of sea-turtle numbers, the dangers they face, and what they need to survive.

Tortuguero National Park in Costa Rica is one of the world's largest protected sea-turtle nesting sites.

ecotourism tourist activities based on respect for nature

Activity Zone!

At Tortuguero National Park, trained local guides give tours of sea-turtle nesting sites to small groups of ecotourists. They are very careful never to disturb the turtles.

Follow these steps to create a *Race for Survival* game to share your knowledge of sea turtles with a friend.

1. Gather important facts about sea turtles from this book. Include facts about how turtles grow and change, how they move around, what they eat, what kinds of dangers they face, and how people help them.

2. Design a board for your game. It could be in the shape of a turtle, or it could look like the sea and the seashore.

3. Design sea-turtle picture counters.

4. Find two dice and a friend, and start playing!

Start

You are the first to hatch from the clutch of eggs. **Take an extra turn.**

You catch a current and ride toward the open sea. **Move ahead 2 spaces.**

A hungry fish tries to catch you. **Miss a turn.**

You reach the ocean at last. **Swim forward 2 spaces.**

Ecotourists provide jobs for locals and help governments realize that protecting endangered animals is worthwhile.

23

Find Out More!

1. What kinds of turtles live in your part of the world? Choose a turtle to study. Find out where it lives, what it eats, and if it is endangered.

2. Many other animals, such as birds, fish, whales, and caribou, also migrate. Pick one and find out why it migrates, how far it travels, and what dangers it faces.

To find out more about the ideas in *Turtle Trouble*, visit www.researchit.org on the web.

Index

eggs	5, 12–17
hatchlings	14–15, 17, 21
marine biologists	11, 19
migration	10–11, 19
nesting	12–13, 18–20, 22–23
nets	16, 18
protection	16–18, 20–23
reptiles	5
species	8–9